Cooking for Heroes

American Red Cross

A Cookbook By
American Red Cross Blood Services
Mid-Atlantic Region & Greater
Chesapeake and Potomac Region

1-800-RED CROSS | redcrossblood.org
(1-800-733-2767)

Special Thanks

Ivy Ammann
Tracy Baccus
Mary Carolino
Cheryl Flanagan
Terry Flanagan
Kathryn Freid
Juan Carlos Gutierrez
Sally Rose Gawne
Lea V. Hagins
Virginia Haidul
Steven Harte, Esq.

John Harte, Sr.
Charlie Hatfield
Sophie & Coulter Hatfield
Debbie Hughes, Esq.
Albert Manzo
Craig Mendelsohn, Esq.
Tamsen Oravetz
Gary J. Ouellette
Shaunna Pickett
Lori Polacheck, Esq.
Paul J. Regal

Madeline Regal
Josie Regal
Lydia Rountree
Tracy Scott
Travis Smaglo
Doug & Gail Stay
Matt Turner
Katie Turner
Julie Whitmer
Charlie Wilcox
Brian Witt

Concept and Layout: Kristen M. Hatfield
Art Direction: Stephanie Stay
©2010 The American National Red Cross   DRD/AP/.1218

I'd like to dedicate this cookbook to all of the blood and platelet donors, blood drive sponsors, volunteers, and all of those who continually support the life-saving mission of the American Red Cross. You help save lives *every* day in our community and we are truly grateful for that.

Please enjoy the recipes that fill these pages. You'll find plenty of delicious appetizers, main dishes, and even some decadent desserts including my own "Fantastic Cheesecake" recipe. I'd also like to thank all of the wonderful celebrities and Red Cross supporters who shared their family recipes and made "Cooking For Heroes" possible. You are all my heroes.

Gary J. Ouellette
CEO, American Red Cross
Greater Chesapeake & Potomac Blood Services Region

American Red Cross

Greater Chesapeake and Potomac
Blood Services Region

The need is constant.
The gratification is instant.
Give blood.™

Starters

American
Red Cross

From the Kitchen of
President Carter and First Lady Rosalynn Carter

"Plains Special" Cheese Ring
A Carter Family Favorite

Ingredients

- 1 lb grated sharp cheddar cheese
- 1 cup mayonnaise
- 1 cup finely chopped nuts
- 1 small onion, finely grated
- Black pepper
- Dash of cayenne
- Strawberry preserves

Instructions

1. Combine all ingredients except preserves, season to taste with pepper.

2. Mix well, mold by hand into a ring and refrigerate until firm for several hours or overnight.

3. Fill center with strawberry preserves and serve with crackers on the side.

Photo Credit: Annemarie Poyo/The Carter Center

"This cheese ring recipe is a favorite in our community. When Jimmy and I were in the Georgia Governor's Mansion, I named it the "Plains Special" Cheese Ring and served it on many occasions - both in the family quarters and for public events.

It was a popular dish at the White House, too. So many people asked for the recipe that we eventually had it printed on cards to handle the requests."

-Rosalynn Carter, former First Lady

From the Kitchen of
Miss USA 2010
Rima Fakih

Tabouli

Ingredients

- 3 cups of finely chopped flat leaf parsley

- ½ cup of finely chopped mint

- 4 or 5 finely chopped spring onions (with the green parts)

- 4 tomatoes, medium size, chopped into small cubes

- 100 g of fine burghul (burghul is a form of whole wheat that has been cleaned, parboiled, dried, ground into particles and sifted into distinct sizes)

- ½ cup lemon juice

- 4 Tbsp olive oil

- Salt and Pepper

Instructions

1. Chop parsley and mint very fine and add to bowl.

2. Repeat with green onions and add to bowl.

3. Chop tomatoes, preferably by hand, into about ¼" dice, and add to bowl.

4. Wash burghul thoroughly, drain, and soak in fresh hot water for about 1 hour.

5. Drain and squeeze as dry as possible, and combine with vegetables.

6. Drizzle with lemon juice and olive oil.

7. Add salt and pepper to taste, and toss thoroughly. You can be quite generous with the pepper.

8. You can make tabouli into a lettuce wrap dish if you like and place the lettuce on the bottom of the bowl, the tabouli on top (optional).

"Since I'm a vegetarian, like to eat healthy, and come from a Lebanese background, I chose a well-known dish called Tabouli. Tabouli is known to be a salad, but it's most definitely not your ordinary salad. I love to eat it alone, or in a pita bread with hummus sometimes."

-Rima Fakih, Miss USA 2010

From the Kitchen of
Bob Barker

Bruschetta
6 Servings

Ingredients

- 6 large, ripe tomatoes (about 2½ pounds), peeled, seeded and cut in ½ inch dice

- Salt and pepper (to personal taste)

- ½ cup tightly packed basil leaves

- 8 garlic cloves, peeled and halved

- 1 cup extra virgin olive oil

- 6 one-inch-thick slices of sourdough or coarse Italian bread

Instructions

1. Place tomatoes in a large bowl and season with salt and pepper. Set aside 6 large basil leaves. Stack the remaining basil leaves. Roll them up and thinly slice them with a sharp knife. Sprinkle over the tomatoes. Add all but 2 pieces of the halved garlic cloves and the olive oil and stir to combine. Set aside to marinate at room temperature for 1 to 2 hours.

2. Grill or toast the slices of bread until well browned. While the toast is hot, rub each slice with the 2 reserved pieces of garlic; the garlic should almost melt into the toast.

3. Pick out the garlic cloves from the tomatoes and discard. Generously spoon the tomato mixture on the toast, making sure to include some olive oil with each spoonful. Garnish each Bruschetta with one of the reserved basil leaves and serve immediately.

From the Kitchen of
Arnold Palmer

Sugared Bacon Strips

Ingredients

- Bacon
  Have at room temperature for best results; ½ lb - 1 lb, depending on desired sweetness

- Brown sugar, approximately 1 cup

Instructions

1. Roll (or pat or shake) raw bacon in brown sugar and place strips on any flat pan with sides.

2. Bake in a slow oven (275° - 300°) for about 25-30 minutes until dark brown. You may turn over once with a pincher or tongs.

3. When bacon appears well done, remove with tongs and DRAIN ON BROWN PAPER very thoroughly (grocery bags are very good for this).

4. As it cools, it will get hard and can then be broken into smaller pieces or served whole. This tedious chore can be done earlier in the day and stored in aluminum foil, then reheated to serve.

Sugared Bacon Strips

From the Kitchen of
John "Boog" Powell

Sweet Vinegar Slaw

Ingredients

- 1 head cabbage, shredded
- 1 onion, thinly sliced
- ¾ cup sugar
- 1 tsp celery seed
- 1 tsp prepared mustard
- 1 cup white vinegar
- 1 tsp sugar
- 1½ tsp salt
- ¾ cup salad oil

Instructions

1. In a large covered dish, alternate layers of cabbage and onion. Sprinkle with sugar.

2. Combine and heat the celery seed, mustard, vinegar, sugar and salt. <u>Do not let mixture boil.</u>

3. When hot, add the salad oil and pour over the cabbage and onions.

4. Cover tightly and refrigerate. It will keep for several weeks in the refrigerator.

"This side dish is excellent with pulled pork, hot dogs, pit beef, fried chicken and just about anything you can think of."

-John "Boog" Powell

From the Kitchen of
Virginia Governor Bob McDonnell

Black Bean Salsa
Bob and Maureen McDonnell

Ingredients

- 1 can of black beans, drained
- 1 can of yellow corn
- 3 tomatoes, diced
- 2 red onions, diced
- 2 jalapeño peppers, minced
- 6 oz of chopped cilantro
- 5 oz of fresh lime juice
- Salt and pepper to taste

Instructions

1. Combine all ingredients and chill for at least 2 hours.
2. Serve with your favorite chips and enjoy!

Pictured from left to right: Ben Jaffe (Tuba), Walter Payton (Bass), Mark Braud (seated, Trumpet), Clint Maedgen (Tenor Sax), Joe Lastie (Drums), Charlie Gabriel (seated, Clarinet), Rickie Monie (Piano), Freddie Lonzo (Trombone).

American Red Cross

You can donate blood every 56 days, 6 times a year.

From the Kitchen of
Ben Jaffe
Preservation Hall
Jazz Band

Ben's New Orleans
Red Beans & Rice
Feeds 16-20

Ingredients

- 2 lb bag of Camellia® Brand Red Kidney Beans

- 1 lb of basmati long grain white rice (or brown rice)

- 3-5 bay leaves (dried)

- Salt and pepper

Instructions

1. Wash red beans thoroughly in a strainer. Let soak in water, with the bay leaves, in a covered pot overnight. Ratio should be 3:1, water to beans.

2. In the morning, bring the water to a boil. Once boiling, reduce the flame to a simmer. Add salt and pepper. For the next 3-5 hours, stir occasionally. BEWARE of burning beans. Do not ever overheat!!!! And, do not stir the beans all the way to the bottom of the pot. You will scrape up burnt beans and ruin the dish!!!!

3. After two hours, begin mashing the beans, with a potato masher, in the pot. The mixture should be watery and thick. Cook until smooth and creamy.

4. Rice: Wash the rice several times until the washing runoff water is clear. Bring a large pot of salted water to boil. Drop in a teaspoon of white wine vinegar. Ratio of 5:1, water to rice. Let rice boil vigorously for 8-12 minutes. Strain the rice.

5. Serve on a plate in a ratio of 2:3, rice to beans. Serve with a fresh green garden salad.

"This is a recipe I learned from my Piran (Creole for Godfather). We used to eat beans every day. Beans and chicken on Monday, beans and sausage on Tuesday, beans and pork chops on Wednesday, beans and meatballs on Thursday and beans and fried catfish on Friday. The trick to New Orleans cooking is patience and time. If you're in a hurry, this dish ISN'T for you."

-Ben Jaffe, Preservation Hall

From the Kitchen of
First Lady Michelle Obama

White House Kitchen Garden Cucumber Soup

Ingredients

- 2 cups almond milk*

- 2 large cucumbers

- 3 oz Greek yogurt

- 2 Tbsp dill

- Salt

- Toasted almonds, Greek yogurt and dill for garnish

If unavailable, prepare the almond milk: Scald two cups of milk with a handful of slivered almonds. Steep 10 minutes. Let cool (leave the almonds in).

Instructions

1. Peel, seed and coarsely chop the cucumbers. Add cucumbers, almond milk, Greek yogurt, dill and salt to blender and puree until smooth.

2. Serve chilled. Garnish with toasted almonds, a dollop of Greek yogurt and a sprig of dill.

American Red Cross

Every 2 seconds someone in the United States needs blood.

From the Kitchen of
Lisa & Patrick Swayze

Chicken-Coconut Soup With Siamese Ginger & Lemon Grass

Ingredients

- 3 cups chicken stock or canned chicken broth

- 8 large slices unpeeled Siamese ginger *(galanga or kha)*, about 5½ oz, or common ginger

- 1 large stalk lemon grass, tough outer leaves discarded, trimmed to 12 inches and angle-cut into 2 inch pieces

- 12 (6 pairs) fresh Kaffir lime leaves *(bai magroot)*, or strips of peel from 1 small lime

- 2 cans (14 oz each) unsweetened coconut milk

- 1 lb boneless, skinless chicken breast, cut into bite-size pieces

- 2 Tbsp *Thai Kitchen Roasted Red Chili Paste* (or any red chili paste)

- ¼ cup fresh lemon juice

- 2½ Tbsp coconut-palm sugar or golden brown sugar

- 2½ Tbsp Thai fish sauce *(nam pla)*

- ½ lb mushrooms, sliced

- 5 small Thai chilies *(phrik khee nu)*, stemmed and lightly crushed

Instructions

1. Put the stock, ginger, and lemon grass in a soup pot. If using Kaffir lime leaves, tear each leaf in half and add to the pot. If using lime peel, add to the pot. Gradually bring the stock to a boil over medium-high heat.

2. Boil for 1 minute, stir in the coconut milk, and return to a boil.

3. Stir in the chicken and return to a boil.

4. Add the chili paste, lemon juice, sugar, and fish sauce. Stir until the chili paste and sugar are dissolved and blended. Add the mushrooms and simmer just until tender, about 1 minute.

5. Float the chilies on top and turn off the heat. Ladle the soup into a steamboat, a soup tureen, or individual serving bowls. Serve with Jasmine Rice.

*The Siamese ginger, lemon grass, and the lime that flavor Thai soups are not meant to be eaten. Eating the chilies is optional.

From the Kitchen of
Alex Trebek

Old Fashioned French-Canadian Pea Soup

Ingredients

- 1 lb salt pork

- 2 large onions (chopped)

- 1 lb whole yellow peas

- 1 carrot (grated or chopped into small pieces)

- 1 lb package of cubed ham

Instructions

1. Soak peas overnight.

2. Rinse a few times then put in a large pot. Cover with water so that the water is 4" over the peas.

3. Add whole salt pork, onions and bring to a gentle boil with the pot cover on until peas are tender or al dente.

4. Add carrots and cubed ham.

5. Season to taste with salt and pepper.

From the Kitchen of
Chef Emeril Lagasse

Green Onion Spoonbread
Makes 8 to 10 servings

Photo by Steven Freeman, 2009

Ingredients

- 3 Tbsp unsalted butter
- 1 cup plus 3 Tbsp stone ground cornmeal
- 1 2/3 cups milk
- 2/3 cup heavy cream
- 2/3 cup buttermilk
- 1 tsp salt
- 1 tsp freshly ground black pepper
- 4 ounces sharp cheddar cheese, grated
- 4 eggs, separated
- ¼ cup finely chopped green onions, green and white parts
- 1 tsp chopped fresh thyme leaves
- 1 tsp baking soda
- 1 tsp baking powder
- 2 tsp sugar

Instructions

1. Butter a 9-inch by 13-inch baking dish with 1 Tbsp of the butter. Add 3 Tbsp of the cornmeal to the pan and tilt the pan to coat the bottom and sides with the cornmeal. Set pan aside.

2. Combine the milk, cream, buttermilk, salt and pepper in a medium saucepan, and bring just to a boil. Whisk in the 1 cup cornmeal and cook, stirring constantly, until cornmeal mixture thickens and is the consistency of grits, 1 to 2 minutes. Remove from the heat and immediately transfer to a heatproof bowl. Stir in the cheese and set the bowl aside until the mixture is lukewarm, stirring often to prevent a skin from forming on the top, 10 to 15 minutes.

3. Preheat the oven to 350° F.

4. In a small bowl, lightly beat the egg yolks, then stir yolks into the cornmeal mixture along with the green onions, thyme, baking soda and baking powder.

5. Combine the egg whites and sugar and beat the whites until stiff peaks form. Fold one-third of the whites into the cornmeal mixture to lighten it. Then gently fold in the remaining whites, taking care not to deflate the whites.

6. Transfer mixture to the prepared baking dish, and bake until the spoonbread is puffed and golden brown on top, and a knife inserted into the center comes out clean, about 30 minutes. Serve immediately.

[Recipe by Emeril Lagasse from *Farm to Fork: Cooking Local, Cooking Fresh* (HarperStudio, 2010), courtesy Martha Stewart Living Omnimedia, Inc.]

"Not much needs to be added to this luscious, moist spoonbread – it is delicious simply with green onions and cheese as an accent. But your imagination can run wild without much risk. Add an abundant herb or another of your favorite ingredients… garlic, crumbled crisp-cooked bacon, corn kernels…"

-Chef Emeril Lagasse

From the Kitchen of
Julian Lennon
Owner of
Blowfish Sushi Restaurant

Fire Oysters

Ingredients

- Malpeque Oyster, 5 pieces

- 1 oz Pesto

- 1 oz Monterey Jack Cheese

- 2 Tbsp Homemade Aioli (Garlic Mayonnaise)

- 0.1 oz Wasabi Tobiko

- ½ tsp Tabasco

Instructions

1. Shuck the oysters.

2. Spread pesto and mayonnaise.

3. Add Monterey Jack Cheese.

4. Cook on grill for approximately 10 minutes.

5. Top with Wasabi Tobiko and Tabasco.

Garnish: Lemon Grass and Kosher Salt.

From the Kitchen of
Natalie Coughlin

Mesclun Salad With California Dried Plums, Goat Cheese and Pecans

Makes 4 Servings

Ingredients

- 2 Tbsp extra virgin olive oil

- 2 tsp balsamic vinegar

- 1 tsp minced shallot

- Salt and black pepper

- 8 cups Mesclun lettuce

- ¾ cup (about 4½ ounces) quartered California pitted dried plums

- ½ cup crumbled goat cheese

- ½ cup candied pecans

Instructions

1. To make vinaigrette, in small bowl, whisk together oil, vinegar and shallot; season with salt and pepper.

2. In large mixing bowl, toss lettuce with enough vinaigrette to coat lightly.

3. Divide among 4 salad plates; sprinkle each salad with 3 tablespoons dried plums, 2 tablespoons goat cheese and 2 tablespoons pecans.

Recipe is courtesy of Olympic and World Champion swimmer Natalie Coughlin and the California Dried Plum Board. Ms. Coughlin is a paid spokesperson for the California Dried Plum Board. For additional recipes, visit http://www.californiadriedplums.org

From the Kitchen of
LeeAnn McCall
American Red Cross Staff

Dwayne's Cornbread
In memory of Dwayne Moseley, from his friends at the Red Cross

Ingredients

- 3 boxes Jiffy® Corn Muffin Mix
- 1 can whole corn, white and yellow
- One 16 oz container of sour cream
- One 12 oz can evaporated milk
- ¾ stick of butter
- 1 egg

Instructions

1. Preheat oven to 400°.

2. Mix corn bread mix, 2/3 container of sour cream, drained corn, egg and milk.

3. Melt the butter in the oven in a 9" x 13" baking pan.

4. Pour mixture into pan. Using spoon, spread the overflow of butter over the top of the cornbread batter.

5. Bake for approximately 30 minutes, until golden brown. Remove from oven and enjoy!

From the Kitchen of
Ernie Smith
American Red Cross Staff

Baked Cheese Enchiladas

Ingredients

- 2 lbs of ground beef
- 1 pack of 10 Flour Tortillas (large ones work better)
- 4 cups Mozzarella cheese
- 4 cups mild or medium cheddar cheese
- Two 8 oz cans Enchilada sauce (mild or hot)
- One 12 oz jar of picante sauce, mild or hot (How HOT do you want it?)
- Optional: mushrooms, jalapeño peppers, chopped onions and sour cream (as a topping)

Instructions

1. Preheat oven to 350°.

2. Brown 1-1½ lbs of ground beef in a skillet, then drain. Return to low-medium heat with a splatter shield. Add two 8 oz cans of hot or mild enchilada sauce and one 16 oz jar of picante hot or mild sauce. You can also add one small can of mushrooms or chopped onions (optional). Stir and let simmer for 10 minutes.

3. In a large mixing bowl, combine cheeses. Place warmed (microwaved) large soft flour tortillas on a plate and place about 1 cup of cheese in middle of tortilla. Fold in half then roll closed and place in 9" x 13" baking dish. Bottom of dish should hold 4-5 filled tortillas and more can be placed on top of bottom layer.

4. Take hamburger sauce from step 2 and pour on top of cheese tortillas slowly and carefully to almost cover. Add any leftover cheese to the top.

5. Bake dish in 350° oven for 30 minutes. Will be hot [temperature] and you may wish to let it sit for a few minutes. Best served with sour cream.

From the Kitchen of
Jodi Hiebert
Blood Donor

Easy Pot Roast

Ingredients

- 2-4 lbs beef roast, boneless chuck works great (trim visible fat)
- 1 can of cream of mushroom soup
- 1 packet of dry onion soup mix
- 1 can or bottle of beer (alcohol gets cooked out)

Instructions

Crock-Pot®:

1. Place beef roast in Crock-Pot®, cover with mushroom soup. Pour over that with the soup mix and beer.

2. Cook on low all day or until tender. Serve roast and gravy with potatoes and vegetables.

Oven:

1. Preheat oven to 400°. Brown roast on stove first in oven-safe pan. Cover with mushroom soup, pour over that with the soup mix and beer. Cover roast and place in oven.

2. After about 15 minutes at 400°, reduce heat to 325°. Bake about 15-20 minutes per pound or until tender. Serve roast and gravy with potatoes and vegetables. Note: Sometimes the gravy needs to be thickened a bit. Use milk or a mixture of flour and water and add slowly to thicken the gravy.

From the Kitchen of
Bridgit Phelps
American Red Cross Staff

Sautéed Spinach

Ingredients

- 2-3 bags fresh spinach (washed and patted dry)
- 2 cloves minced garlic
- ¼ cup white wine (or enough to keep the spinach moist while cooking)

Instructions

1. Heat garlic and half of the wine in a large nonstick pan on medium high heat until garlic is lightly brown. Stir for about 1 minute.

2. Add spinach in batches. As the spinach wilts add more until all spinach has been added.

3. Add remaining wine. Stir to mix spinach evenly with wine and garlic.

4. Cover and reduce heat to low. Simmer for about 2-3 minutes until all spinach is wilted and warmed throughout.

5. Serve immediately! This goes great with grilled pork or chicken.

From the Kitchen of
Mary Carolino
Blood and Platelet Recipient

Spanikopita (Spinach Pie)

Ingredients

- ½ package of Phyllo (Fillo)
- 1 stick of melted butter
- 1 medium onion, chopped
- 30 oz of frozen chopped spinach
- 1 lb feta cheese
- 6 eggs
- 2 Tbsp dill weed
- ½ tsp salt
- ½ tsp pepper

Instructions

1. Most fillo packages have two sleeves of twenty 9" x 14" pastry leaves. Defrost one sleeve in the refrigerator overnight. If package only has one sleeve of larger leaves, you can still use 20 leaves, but you may need to trim before baking. Fillo tends to dry out very quickly, so do not open the package until you are ready to assemble.

2. Drain chopped spinach as it defrosts.

3. Heat oven to 350°. Butter a 9" x 13" baking dish.

4. Sauté chopped onions in 2 Tbsp of butter until they start to turn clear and add dill weed for the last minute.

5. In a large bowl, mix eggs, feta, salt and pepper. Squeeze any excess liquid out of the spinach and add to the egg mixture. Stir in sauteed onions/dill weed and mix everything well.

6. Use half of the fillo on the bottom of the baking dish, layering 2 sheets at a time and brushing thoroughly with melted butter between layers.

7. Pour spinach mixture on top of fillo and cover with remaining fillo in the same manner including the top layer.

8. Cook for 45 minutes or until top is a light golden brown. Cut into 3" squares and serve warm (although cold leftovers make a yummy breakfast!).

Platelets, critical for cancer patients, have a shelf life of only 5 days.

Ukrainian Borscht

Ingredients

- 2 lbs soup beef with cracked bones
- 2½ quarts cold water
- 1 lb lean fresh pork
- 2 lbs smoked pork
- 1 bay leaf
- 10 peppercorns
- 1 clove garlic
- 1 bunch fresh parsley, coarsely chopped
- 1 carrot, sliced
- 1 stalk celery, sliced
- 1 leek, sliced
- 8 medium beets
- 3 Tbsp cold water
- 1 cup shredded cabbage
- 2 large onions, quartered
- 3 large potatoes, cut in eighths
- ¼ cup tomato purée
- 2 Tbsp vinegar
- 2 tsp sugar
- 1 can navy beans
- 5 sausages, sliced thick
- Salt
- Sour cream (optional)

Instructions

1. In a heavy six-quart pot, simmer the beef and bone in the water about one hour.

2. Add the fresh and smoked pork. Add the next 7 ingredients. Cover tightly and bring to a boil, reduce heat and simmer 1½ hours.

3. Meanwhile, boil seven of the beets, unpeeled, until tender. Slip off the skins and cut each into eight pieces. Grate the eighth beet raw and mix with 3 Tbsp cold water. Reserve.

4. Remove the bones and meats from the pot and discard the bone. Strain the soup, discarding the vegetables and flavoring materials.

5. Slice or shred the meats. Return the meats and liquid to the pot.

6. Add the cooked beets, cabbage, onions, potatoes, tomato purée, vinegar, and sugar.

7. Simmer covered, 45 minutes.

8. Add the beans and sausage and simmer, covered, 10 minutes.

9. Skim the excess fat from the soup. Add the liquid from the grated raw beet and season with salt to taste. Serve hot with optional sour cream.

Note: For sausages, try frankfurters or knockwurst.

From the Kitchen of

Amy Calhoun
Mother of Blood Recipient

Mediterranean Pinwheels

Ingredients

- 8 oz reduced-fat cream cheese, softened
- 2 Tbsp reduced fat sour cream
- 6 oz feta cheese, crumbled
- 1 clove garlic, pressed
- ¼ tsp ground black pepper
- ½ tsp dried oregano
- Zest of one lemon
- Juice of half a lemon
- 2 oz pimentos, chopped and drained
- 1/3 cup Kalamata Olives, chopped fine
- ½ of a cucumber, peeled, seeded and chopped fine
- 10 tortillas, whole wheat or plain flour tortillas
- 5 oz fresh baby spinach leaves, stems removed

Instructions

1. In a small bowl, beat cream cheese, sour cream, and feta with electric mixer until well blended. Then add pressed garlic, black pepper, oregano, lemon zest and lemon juice and blend with mixer until mixed well. Add drained pimentos, olives and chopped cucumbers and stir until mixed well.

2. Spread a thin layer of mix on tortilla leaving about a half an inch around the sides. Top with a layer of spinach.

3. Roll tortilla tightly. Chill for 2- 24 hours. Slice crosswise into bite-size pieces and serve.

Variations:

- Roll like a burrito and have as a sandwich wrap.
- Add your favorite lunch meat.
- Add favorite vegetables, sliced thin or chopped so they'll roll nicely.

From the Kitchen of

Kim Thomas
American Red Cross Staff

Stuffed Mushrooms

Ingredients

- 2 cartons of mushrooms of your choice, whole stem removed and washed
- One 8 oz package of cream cheese, softened
- 1 package of real bacon bits
- One container 16 oz sour cream
- 1 small Vidalia onion chopped very fine, minced
- 2 cups of shredded mixed cheese
- 1 envelope of onion soup mix
- 1 tsp garlic powder

Instructions

1. Preheat oven to 375°.

2. Mix all of the ingredients together in a large bowl with a firm-handled spoon.

3. Coat a 9"x13" glass baking dish with pan spray.

4. Overstuff each mushroom and place in baking dish.

5. Bake for 30 minutes, depending on oven. Once the mushrooms begin to brown, sprinkle with additional cheese and brown on broil to your liking.

From the Kitchen of
Rebecca Crosen
Blood Recipient

Quick Pea Salad

Ingredients

- 1 head of lettuce (chopped)
- 1 large bag of FROZEN peas
- ½ medium size red onion
- 4 chopped celery stalks
- 4 cups shredded sharp cheddar cheese
- 1 cup of chopped bacon pieces (real bacon)
- 2 cups (or to taste) Miracle Whip®

Instructions

1. It's important to layer this dish correctly so that the lettuce doesn't wilt. In a large bowl, your first layer is the chopped head of lettuce.

2. Then layer in the FROZEN peas. It is critical that the peas remain frozen.

3. After the peas, add the celery and red onion then spread the Miracle Whip® in a thick layer this will keep the peas cool and the lettuce from wilting.

4. On top of the Miracle Whip® layer, nicely add the layer of cheese and bacon last.

5. You can add more cheese or Miracle Whip® to taste, but do NOT mix the ingredients until you are ready to serve. Keep refrigerated when not serving and enjoy!

From the Kitchen of
Sylvia Howard
Blood Donor

Executive Salad

Ingredients

- Small head of lettuce
- ½ cup chopped celery
- Small can of green peas
- 1 lb bacon (I use bacon bits)
- 1 cup mayonnaise
- 1 cup chopped green pepper
- 3 boiled eggs
- 1 small can of grated cheese
- 1 Tbsp sugar
- 2 or 3 medium tomatoes chopped

Instructions

1. Line dish with lettuce.

2. Layer all vegetables.

3. Drain peas and spread over vegetables.

4. Spread mayonnaise over all.

5. Sprinkle sugar.

6. Sprinkle cheese.

7. Refrigerate overnight.

8. The next day, sprinkle chopped eggs, tomatoes and bacon bits. Delicious!

a drop of humor   by Charlie Hatfield

"When you are O negative, you're EVERYBODY'S type!"

Main Dishes

American Red Cross

From the Kitchen of
First Lady Michelle Obama

Obama Family Chili

Ingredients

- 1 large onion, chopped
- 1 green pepper, chopped
- Several cloves of garlic, chopped
- 1 Tbsp olive oil
- 1 lb ground turkey or beef
- ¼ tsp ground cumin
- ¼ tsp ground oregano
- ¼ tsp ground turmeric
- ¼ tsp ground basil
- 1 Tbsp chili powder
- 3 Tbsp red wine vinegar
- Several tomatoes, depending on size, chopped
- 1 can red kidney beans

Instructions

1. Sauté onions, green pepper and garlic in olive oil until soft. Add ground meat and brown.

2. Combine spices together into a mixture, then add to ground meat. Add red wine vinegar.

3. Add tomatoes and let simmer, until tomatoes cook down.

4. Add kidney beans and cook for a few minutes.

5. Serve over white rice.

6. Garnish with grated cheddar cheese, onions and sour cream.

From the Kitchen of
Tina Knowles, Beyoncé's Mother

Tina's Creole Gumbo
Serves 12

Ingredients

- Approximately 1 cup of vegetable oil
- 2½ cups of flour
- 6 one-pound bags of cut frozen okra
- 1 Tbsp of vinegar
- 3 gallons of water
- ½ bunch of celery, chopped
- 3 large bell peppers (any color), chopped
- 4 yellow onions, chopped
- 3 bunches of green onions, chopped
- 1½ cups of McCormick® seasoning salt
- ¼ cup of garlic powder
- ¼ cup of accent seasoning
- 4 Tbsp of cayenne pepper
- 4 Tbsp of black pepper
- 1 dozen medium-size crabs, or 1½ dozen small crabs, cleaned but still in the shell
- 6 large chicken breasts cut into chunks
- 15 large chicken drumsticks
- 1 16 oz can of tomatoes, diced
- 6 lbs of beef sausage, sliced into disks
- 6 lbs of uncooked medium-size shrimp, peeled and deveined
- Rice (follow instructions on box for the desired amount)

Instructions

1. To make the roux: Pour the vegetable oil into a skillet so that the bottom is covered and heat over medium to medium-high heat. Add the flour a little at a time until it's all blended. Add the rest of the oil as needed. Stir constantly until its browned to a dark fudge consistency. You know you are rockin' the roux when it changes from a peanut-butter shade to a dark chocolate color. This takes about 45 minutes. The key to roux is not to scorch it. If the roux starts to get darker than a peanut butter color before a half hour passed, the heat is too high. If that happens, remove the pan from the stove, still stirring and turn down the heat a little. Let the burner cool down for a while before placing the pan back on the stove. It may take some experimenting before you find the right setting. If you burn the roux it will kill the taste of your gumbo, so you'll have to throw it away, clean the utensils and start all over.

2. In another skillet, fry the okra. The secret is to cook the okra so that when you add it to your gumbo it isn't slimy and mushy. Cover the bottom of the skillet with about 3 tablespoons of oil and heat over low to medium heat. Add the okra. Then add about a teaspoon of vinegar (this cuts down on the slime) and continue to stir-fry the okra. Whenever you see it getting a little slimy, add a splash of vinegar. Also add oil to prevent sticking as needed. You don't want to cook it to death, so I'd say no more than 15 minutes frying time for a whole bag.

3. To make the gumbo: Pour the water into a large gumbo pot and add celery, bell peppers, onions, green onions and all the seasonings. You do not want to boil the vegetables. You want to slow-cook them so that the flavor comes out, so set your stove on low to medium heat and leave it there while you add the crabs, chicken, tomatoes, sausage and cooked okra. Pour in the roux, but stir gently as you add it to make sure that it separates into the water evenly. Taste to check the seasoning. To make it less spicy, add more water, or to make it spicier, add more of the seasonings. Simmer, covered, over low to medium heat for three to four hours or until the meat is nice and tender, and the flavor is rich and robust. There are no shortcuts, so you are going to have to baby-sit that pot until it's ready. Stir it frequently with an extra long spoon that reaches to the bottom of the pot. Add the shrimp a few minutes before the gumbo is served. They will turn pink when done.

4. Serve over rice.

From the Kitchen of
Wayne Gretzky

Grandma Gretzky's Famous Meatloaf
Serves 5 (Prep Time: 20 minutes; Cook Time: 99 minutes)

Ingredients

- 80 oz (5 lbs) Ground Chuck Sirloin (Certified Angus)
- 3 Eggs (medium)
- 2 oz Dijon mustard (1 oz reserved)
- .75 fl oz tabasco sauce
- .75 fl oz Worcestershire sauce
- .5 oz cajun spice
- 10 pinches salt
- 7 pinches black pepper, ground
- ½ Tbsp oregano, dry
- ½ Tbsp thyme, dry
- 4 oz French Onion Soup Mix, dry
- 3 oz fresh garlic, minced
- 2 oz bread crumbs

Sauce
- 8 oz Spanish onions (peeled and Julienne)
- 8 oz Demi Glace or good quality beef stock
- ½ Tbsp fresh thyme, chopped
- ½ Tbsp fresh rosemary, chopped
- 1.5 oz red wine
- ½ clove crushed garlic

Instructions

1. Preheat convection oven to 350° F – or about the same temperature as a Stanley Cup Final game!

2. In a large mixing bowl gently beat eggs and add 1 oz Dijon mustard and all ingredients. Use a mixer (not the McSorley type) with a stiff paddle, if available, until all ingredients are mixed together.

3. Line a meatloaf pan with parchment paper and spray the paper with cooking spray. Pat beef mixture into the insert pan, packing it in tightly. Brush the remaining 1 oz Dijon mustard on the top of the loaf.

4. Cover the loaf first with plastic wrap, then with aluminum foil (shiny side down). Place the loaf on a baking tray and bake in convection oven at 350° F for 99 minutes! If non-convection oven, bake until internal temperature reaches 180° F.

5. To make sauce, heat oil in large frying pan and add onions. Continue cooking onions, adding garlic, on medium-high heat until caramelized (golden brown). Add red wine and reduce by half. Add herbs and stock and let simmer for 20 minutes or until thickened.

6. When meatloaf is done let cool for 20 minutes (or two 10 minute misconducts!) and carefully remove from pan. Serve with mashed potatoes and your favorite vegetables. Ladle sauce over meatloaf, slice and serve.

"This was a family favorite in my household growing up. It is also a dish that is proudly served at my restaurant in Toronto."

-Wayne Gretzky

From the Kitchen of
Mario Lopez

Mac & Cheese
Serves 6

Ingredients

- 1 lb whole grain elbow macaroni (like Whole Wheat Barilla PLUS® or Tinkyáda® Brown Rice Pasta)

- 1 Tbsp unsalted butter

- ½ cup diced onion

- ½ tsp kosher salt

- ½ tsp black pepper

- ½ tsp Worcestershire sauce

- 1 Tbsp all-purpose flour

- 1 cup low fat (1%) milk

- 2 Tbsp reduced fat cream cheese (Neufchatel cheese)

- 1 cup shredded cheddar cheese

- Pinch of ground nutmeg

- 1 cup chopped roasted red peppers

- Nonstick cooking spray

- 1 slice whole wheat bread

- 2 Tbsp grated Parmesan cheese

- 1 tsp olive oil

- 1 clove garlic

Instructions

1. Preheat oven to 350°.

2. Cook pasta according to package directions.

3. While pasta is cooking, melt butter in a large saucepan.

4. Add onion, salt, pepper, and Worcestershire sauce, and sauté for 5 minutes.

5. Sprinkle flour over onions and cook, stirring constantly for 1 minute.

6. Whisk in milk and simmer until thickened.

7. Stir in cream cheese, cheddar, and nutmeg and cook until cheese is melted—turn off heat.

8. Add drained pasta to cheese mixture along with roasted peppers and mix well.

9. Transfer to a baking dish sprayed with nonstick cooking spray.

10. For the topping, place bread, cheese, oil, and garlic in a food processor fitted with a steel blade; pulse until bread is in fine crumbs.

11. Sprinkle bread crumbs over pasta and bake for 10 minutes until golden.

[REPRINTED FROM 'Extra Lean: The Fat-Burning Plan That Changes the Way You Eat for Life' by Mario Lopez with Jimmy Pena, published by Celebra, May 2010]

From the Kitchen of
Doris Roberts

Doris Roberts' Lasagna

Ingredients

- 4 Italian sausages

- 1 lb fresh white button mushrooms, sliced

- 1 cup frozen peas

- 2 packages lasagna noodles

- 6 hard-boiled eggs, sliced into disks

- Meatballs
  (see recipe on next page)

- 1 large container ricotta cheese

- 1 lb mozzarella cheese, shredded

- 1 cup Parmesan cheese, grated

- Meat sauce
  (see recipe on next page)

[REPRINTED FROM *'Are You Hungry Dear?'*
by Doris Roberts, published by
St. Martin's Griffin, 2004]

Instructions

1. In a sauté pan, fry sausages until cooked through. When cool, slice and set aside. Sauté mushrooms and peas in butter, salt, and pepper until soft and mushrooms are starting to brown. Set aside.

2. Cook noodles according to package. Drain, separate, and set aside.

3. Slice eggs and set aside.

4. In a fairly deep baking dish, ladle a thin layer of sauce on the bottom. (The layer of sauce should be only enough to keep the first layer of noodles from sticking to the dish.) Line the dish horizontally with noodles, allowing a generous overhang. Spoon on a bit more sauce and arrange another layer of noodles vertically, as you would do if you were making a lattice pie crust. You'll use the noodles that hang over the sides of the dish to wrap the lasagna when you're finished building the layers, scatter a layer of meatballs onto the noodles. (Be sure to mind the amount of residual sauce that is spooned with the meatballs, as too much sauce will make the dish runny and unable to maintain its shape on the dinner plate.) Add sliced sausage, egg slices, mushrooms, and peas on top of the meatballs. Drop generous dollops of ricotta, followed by a handful of shredded mozzarella and a sprinkling of the Parmesan cheese. Repeat layers until the dish is full. This should give you three substantial layers. When construction is complete, fold the horizontal noodles over the top of the dish. Finish with a layer of sauce and some more Parmesan. Beat one egg vigorously and pour it over the finished lasagna to keep your masterpiece together. Tap dish on countertop to settle layers. Bake at 325° for 30-40 minutes.

"Note: In the spirit of Marie Barone, if you're giving this recipe to your daughter-in-law, leave out the peas, mushrooms, and hard-boiled eggs. She will be unable to answer your son's questions about why it doesn't taste as good as Mom's."

-Doris Roberts

From the Kitchen of
Doris Roberts

Doris' Meatballs

Ingredients

- 2 lbs ground sirloin
- 4 cloves garlic, minced
- 1 cup Parmesan cheese
- 1 handful chopped Italian parsley
- 2 eggs
- Vegetable oil
- Salt and pepper to taste

Instructions

1. Thoroughly mix all ingredients (except oil) in bowl and form into balls about the size of a quarter.

2. Heat 1-1½ inches of vegetable oil. When oil sizzles as a drop of water is added, add meatballs and fry until brown.

3. Transfer to meat sauce (see recipe below).

[REPRINTED FROM *'Are You Hungry Dear?'* by Doris Roberts, published by St. Martin's Griffin, 2004]

Doris' Meat Sauce

Ingredients

- 1 large onion, chopped
- 4 cloves garlic, chopped
- 2 Tbsp basil
- 1 Tbsp parsley
- 1 healthy pinch oregano
- Salt and pepper to taste
- 1 lb ground beef
- Two 28 oz cans whole tomatoes with basil
- 1 can tomato paste

Instructions

1. Cover the bottom of a large pan with good olive oil, not that cheap crap from the 99-cent store, and turn the heat under it to medium. When the oil becomes fragrant, it's warm enough to add the garlic.

2. Add the garlic, the onion, basil, parsley, oregano, salt, and pepper. Sauté until onion is golden.

3. Add the meat and cook until brown, breaking it apart with a wooden spoon.

4. Add the tomatoes, crushing the whole tomatoes by hand. Cover and lower the heat, stirring occasionally for 15 minutes. Continue cooking uncovered for another 15 minutes. Serve over your favorite pasta.

[REPRINTED FROM *'Are You Hungry Dear?'* by Doris Roberts, published by St. Martin's Griffin, 2004]

From the Kitchen of
Patricia Richardson

Pat's Spaghetti Sauce

Ingredients

- 1 large can of whole tomatoes (I use organic)

- 1 can of tomato paste (also organic if possible)

- 3 Tbsp Worcestershire Sauce

- 3 Tbsp Balsamic Vinegar

- Dashes of tabasco (you decide)

- 1 yellow pepper, cut up

- 1 green pepper, cut up

- ½-1 onion, cut up (your preference on the amount of onion)

- Garlic cloves, pressed/cut

- 2-3 stalks of celery, cut up

- Mushrooms, sliced (optional, or if you are doubling recipe and freezing some you might not want to include)

- Fresh basil (you might get whole tomatoes and tomato paste with basil included) oregano, thyme (Italian seasonings), salt, pepper

- ¼ cup sugar

Instructions

1. Bring to a boil, then cover and simmer on LOW for three hours. Stir regularly.

2. Brown 1 lb of ground sirloin or ground turkey. Drain and add to mixture.

3. Cook one more hour. Serve with favorite spaghetti, or whichever pasta you feel like serving it with.

Note: I would always suggest doubling the recipe and sticking some in the freezer. It's so nice to pull it out for another dinner when you don't feel like cooking and you can just thaw it and reheat it, cook some noodles, make a salad and some garlic bread. When you make the garlic bread, melt some butter with a LITTLE Worcestershire sauce in it in addition to the garlic, pour it over your garlic bread before you put it in the oven.

From Left: Ann Bales, Cathy Moseley, Lynn Richardson (Ambrose), and Patricia Richardson

"One of the four things I cook (which I learned from my mother, who cooked like four things other than frozen food) was a spaghetti sauce recipe that me and my three sisters all still cook in mass quantities every time we have family reunions. It is a family favorite and my friends all seem to love it unless they are just being nice and feeling sorry for me because cooking is not my strength."

-Patricia Richardson

From the Kitchen of
Susan Lucci

Chicken Delight
By Helmut Huber & Susan Lucci
Serves 2

Ingredients

- Two chicken breasts

- 10 oz jar Marinara Sauce (preferably Rao's®)

- 3 Tbsp chopped onions

- 1 tsp finely chopped garlic

- 6 mushrooms, cubed

- 10 oz cooked ziti pasta

- Olive oil

- Flour

- Salt and pepper to taste

Instructions

1. Sprinkle salt and pepper on chicken to taste. Slightly dust chicken with flour on both sides.

2. Add 1 Tbsp olive oil to skillet. Preheat then add chicken. Brown chicken on both sides then remove from skillet.

3. Add onions, garlic and mushrooms to skillet. Slightly sauté without browning. Immediately add marinara sauce. Mix thoroughly.

4. Add chicken breasts to sauce mixture. Cover with lid.

5. Preheat oven to 375°. Bake for 15 minutes.

6. Prepare pasta by adding 1 Tbsp olive oil to water to prevent pasta from sticking. Add ziti to boiling water. Cook for approximately 12 minutes.

7. Sprinkle With Parmesan Cheese (if desired) and enjoy!

From the Kitchen of
Caroline Manzo

Veal Piccata (Veal In Lemon Sauce)
Serves About 4

Ingredients

- 1 lb veal cutlets
- ¼ cup flour
- 3 Tbsp olive oil
- 3 Tbsp butter
- 3 Tbsp lemon juice
- Minced parsley, salt, pepper (eyeball it)

Instructions

1. Make sure you pound the veal THIN. Take the flour, add salt & pepper mix it up and dredge the veal in it.

2. Heat the oil and add butter in skillet. Let it "percolate," you want a little sizzle to it.

3. Add the veal, sauté until light golden brown on both sides. Remove veal from pan, skim off the fat from skillet and add parsley and lemon juice.

4. Return the veal into pan and on a low heat coat the veal with lemon juice.

Spaghetti Aglio e Olio (Spaghetti with Oil, Garlic and Parsley)
Serves 4

Ingredients

- 1 lb spaghettini/angel hair (thin spaghetti), cooked and drained
- ½ cup olive oil
- 4-5 whole cloves garlic (the bigger, the better)
- ¼ cup minced parsley

Instructions

1. Heat the oil in a skillet. Add garlic and sauté until golden brown.

2. Pour olive oil over cooked pasta, add parsley and start eating!!!

P.S. I also like to add fresh grated Locatelli cheese and hot pepper flakes to give it a little extra kick!

"This is my boys' favorite!"

-Caroline Manzo, The Real Housewives of New Jersey

From the Kitchen of
Frankie Avalon

Pasta 'n Peas

Ingredients

- 1 Tbsp olive oil
- 1 onion, chopped
- 2-3 cloves garlic
- 1 can garbanzo beans
- 1 box frozen peas
- 1 28 oz can crushed tomatoes
- 2 cups dry Sherry
- 2 cups sweet, red Vermouth
- 1 lb pasta shells
- Oregano
- Pepper

Instructions

1. In a saucepan, sauté together oil, onion and garlic. Add garbanzo beans, frozen peas, tomatoes, Sherry and Vermouth. Stir together, reduce heat to medium-low and let cook for 45 minutes.

2. Fill a large pot (a little more than ¼ full) with water. When water begins to boil, add pasta shells and cook until al dente. You will not need to drain water.

3. Pour tomato sauce into large pot of pasta.

4. Enjoy!

**American
Red Cross**

Type O-negative blood (red cells)
can be transfused to patients of all
blood types. It is always in great
demand and often in short supply.

From the Kitchen of
Yogi & Carmen Berra

Baked Ziti

Ingredients

- ¼ cup olive oil
- 1 onion, chopped
- 3 Tbsp basil, dried or fresh
- 3 Tbsp fresh parsley, chopped
- 2 large cloves garlic, chopped
- ½ lb ground sirloin (optional)
- 1 pinch red pepper
- ½ cup dry red wine
- 1 can (16 oz) crushed tomatoes
- ½ cup shredded Gruyère cheese
- ½ cup shredded Fontina cheese
- ½ cup shredded Mozzarella cheese
- ½ cup shredded Parmesan cheese
- 12 oz Ziti, cooked al dente, drained

Instructions

1. Sauté first 7 ingredients until lightly brown, add wine and simmer 10 minutes.

2. Add tomatoes and cook another 20 minutes.

3. Place pasta in buttered casserole and cover with sauce and cheeses.

4. Bake in 400° oven about 25 minutes.

5. Serve hot with extra Parmesan cheese.

From the Kitchen of

Peter Facinelli

Chicken Francese

Ingredients

- Eggs
- Milk
- Skinless chicken breasts
- Butter
- Lemon
- White cooking wine
- Flour
- Olive oil
- Chicken bouillon
- Parsley

Instructions

1. In a bowl, beat egg and add a little milk. Dip chicken breasts in flour then dip floured chicken into egg mixture.

2. In skillet, heat olive oil (just enough to cover bottom of pan). When oil is hot, put chicken in pan and sear for about a minute on each side. Take chicken out of skillet, dump oil, and wipe pan clean.

3. Add a tablespoon of butter to skillet. When butter is melted, put chicken back in pan over medium flame. Squeeze lemon over chicken, add ½ cup of white wine, one bouillon cube, and water if needed.* Cover with a lid. Turn flame to low and cook for 10-15 minutes.

4. Garnish with parsley. Mangia tutti.

Add small amounts of water to keep the dish moist if white wine evaporates.

You can substitute chicken with a white fish such as Orange Roughy. With fish, do not dip in egg. Just dip into milk then flour and continue with recipe.

From the Kitchen of
Fabian

Scaloppine di Pollo al Pisselli
(Chicken Breasts with Sage and Peas)

Ingredients

- 1 lb boneless and skinless chicken breast

- Salt and freshly ground black pepper

- 2 Tbsp unsalted butter

- 2 Tbsp olive oil

- 12 fresh sage leaves (more, if small)

- 1 cup partially thawed frozen peas

- 1-2 Tbsp lemon juice

Instructions

1. Cut breast into 4 equal portions (more or less), place between 2 sheets of plastic wrap and pound to about ¼ inch thick. Sprinkle each side with salt and pepper.

2. Melt butter with olive oil in large skillet over medium heat. Add chicken and sage to pan. Cook each side until golden brown, remove chicken from pan and keep warm.

3. Add peas and lemon juice to pan and stir. Add salt and pepper to taste. Cover and cook 5 minutes on low.

4. Return chicken to pan, cook, turning until heated through. Serve.

From the Kitchen of
Miss America 2010
Caressa Cameron

Fried Hamburgers
With Mushroom Gravy
Serves 4

Ingredients

- 1 to 1¼ lbs extra lean ground beef

- ¼ tsp ground pepper

- ½ tsp salt

- ¼ tsp seasoned salt

- 3 Tbsp fine dry bread crumbs

- 2 Tbsp milk

- 1 large egg, slightly beaten

- 2 Tbsp grated onion

- 2 Tbsp vegetable oil

- ¾ to 1 cup thinly sliced mushrooms

- 2 Tbsp flour

- 1 cup beef broth

- 1 Tbsp dry red wine, optional

Instructions

1. Combine ground beef, pepper, salt, seasoned salt, and bread crumbs; shape into 4 oval patties.

2. Heat oil in a skillet over medium heat; fry the patties for about 5 minutes on each side, or until cooked through.

3. Remove patties to warm plate and keep warm.

4. Pour off all but about 2 tablespoons of the drippings. Add mushrooms to the drippings and cook until tender.

5. Add flour to the skillet; stir until hot and bubbly. Add the beef broth and wine, if using; cook, stirring, until the sauce is thickened.

6. Pour over the burgers and serve with rice and a vegetable side dish.

"Serve these tasty burgers with rice and your choice of vegetable. Add a little red wine to the gravy for even more flavor."

-Caressa Cameron, Miss America 2010

From the Kitchen of
Joan Collins

Miso Marinated Salmon Served With Toasted Sesame Rice and Cucumber Ribbons

Miso Salmon Ingredients:

- 3 Tbsp white miso paste
- 3 Tbsp rice wine vinegar
- 2 salmon fillets (use tweezers to remove any bones)

Miso Salmon Reduction Ingredients:

- 2 Tbsp white miso paste
- 2 Tbsp rice wine vinegar
- 2 Tbsp caster sugar
- Splash of sake, mirin or vodka

Cucumber Ribbons Ingredients:

- ½ cucumber
- 2 tsp rice wine vinegar
- 1 tsp vegetable oil
- Pinch of caster sugar

Sesame Rice Ingredients:

- ¾ cup long grain rice
- 1½ cups water
- 2 tsp finely grated ginger
- ½ small red chili
- 1 Tbsp sesame seeds, toasted

Miso Salmon Instructions

1. Combine two ingredients into a marinade and spread over salmon so the fillets are evenly coated. Marinade for up to an hour.

2. Lightly oil aluminum foil and grill on gas BBQ or place on cooking sheet and roast in pre-heated 350° oven for 12 minutes.

Miso Salmon Reduction Instructions

1. Combine ingredients in saucepan to create a smooth paste.

2. On medium-high/high heat, bring to a boil.

3. Turn down heat to medium and simmer until it thickens into a glaze.

4. Top the grilled salmon with this glaze.

Cucumber Ribbons Instructions

1. Using a vegetable peeler, shave the cucumber into long, thin ribbons.

2. Whisk together rice wine vinegar, oil and sugar.

3. Toss ribbons in the dressing. Twirl ribbons and mount on plate.

Sesame Rice Instructions

1. Place rice, water, ginger, chili in a small saucepan over high heat and bring to a boil.

2. Reduce heat to low, cover and cook for 15-20 minutes or until rice is cooked.

3. Fluff up with a fork, discard chili and stir through sesame seeds.

4. Spoon into a teacup and turn over on plate.

5. Sprinkle additional sesame seeds on top.

Justin Chon

Chicken Scramble
Serves 6

Ingredients

- 8 egg whites
- 3 oz chicken breast
- ¼ cup of bell peppers
- ¼ cup of onions
- Handful of cheese
- 1 Tbsp olive oil
- Green salsa

Instructions

1. Cook chicken first in a skillet pan with olive oil.

2. Toss in the egg whites.

3. Throw in ¼ cup of bell peppers and ¼ cup of onions.

4. Put it on a plate then sprinkle cheese on the scramble and add some green salsa.

"This makes a hearty and delicious breakfast."

-Justin Chon

From the Kitchen of
Chef Emeril Lagasse

Cheesy Creole Tomato Pie
Makes 6 to 8 servings

Ingredients

- 1 recipe Savory Pie Crust dough (recipe follows on next page)

- 1 egg, separated

- 2 lbs ripe Creole tomatoes or other regional variety, such as heirlooms or beefsteak

- ½ tsp salt

- ¼ tsp freshly ground black pepper

- 4 Tbsp mayonnaise

- 1/3 cup unseasoned dry breadcrumbs

- ¾ cup thinly sliced Vidalia onions

- 1 Tbsp fresh thyme leaves

- 2 Tbsp thinly sliced fresh basil leaves

- 2 oz Fontina cheese, grated (about ½ cup)

- 2 oz mozzarella cheese, grated (about ½ cup)

- 2 Tbsp extra-virgin olive oil

- 2 Tbsp grated Parmigiano Reggiano cheese

[Recipe by Emeril Lagasse from *Farm to Fork: Cooking Local, Cooking Fresh* (HarperStudio, 2010), courtesy Martha Stewart Living Omnimedia, Inc.]

Instructions

1. Roll out the pie dough on a lightly floured surface to fit a 9-inch or 10-inch deep-dish pie plate. Fit the dough into the pie plate and crimp the edges decoratively. Refrigerate, covered, for at least 30 minutes or up to a day.

2. Preheat the oven to 375°F.

3. Remove the pie shell from the refrigerator and line it with aluminum foil. Fill the shell with ceramic pie weights or dried beans, and bake for 13 minutes, or until lightly golden around the edges. Remove the foil and weights, return the shell to the oven, and bake for 3 minutes.

4. Remove the pie crust from the oven and place it on a wire rack. Lightly beat the egg white with a fork. Using a pastry brush, lightly coat the entire surface of the warm pie crust with the egg white (you will probably not use all the white). Then allow the pie shell to cool and the white to set. It will look glazed.

5. Slice the tomatoes into ¼-inch-thick rounds, discarding the stem and root ends. Season the tomatoes with the salt and pepper.

6. Combine the mayonnaise with the egg yolk in a small bowl, and stir until smooth.

7. Sprinkle one third of the breadcrumbs over the bottom of the cooled pie crust. Layer half of the sliced tomatoes over the breadcrumbs in a circular pattern, and top with half of the sliced onions. Drizzle in half of the mayonnaise mixture, and top with half of the herbs, half of the Fontina, half of the mozzarella, and half of the remaining breadcrumbs. Make a second layer with the remaining tomato slices, onions, mayonnaise mixture, herbs, Fontina, mozzarella, and breadcrumbs. Drizzle the olive oil over the top, and sprinkle with the Parmesan cheese.

8. Bake the pie in the oven for 50 minutes to 1 hour, until it is bubbly hot and golden brown. Allow it to cool for at least 30 minutes or up to 5 hours before serving. This pie is at its best at room temperature.

"Have too many ready-to-pick tomatoes in your garden? Try this pie, where the most delicious tomatoes are layered with cheese, sweet onions, breadcrumbs and herbs."

-Chef Emeril Lagasse

From the Kitchen of
Chef Emeril Lagasse

Savory Pie Crust

Makes one 9-inch or 10-inch pie shell

Ingredients

- 1 ¼ cups all-purpose flour

- 1 tsp salt

- ½ tsp freshly ground black pepper

- 8 Tbsp (1 stick) cold unsalted butter, cut into pieces

- 3 to 4 Tbsp ice water

[Recipe by Emeril Lagasse from *Farm to Fork: Cooking Local, Cooking Fresh* (HarperStudio, 2010), courtesy Martha Stewart Living Omnimedia, Inc.]

Instructions

1. Place the flour, salt, and pepper in the bowl of a food processor, and pulse to combine. Add the butter and process until the mixture resembles coarse crumbs. While the machine is running, gradually drizzle in the water, processing until the dough comes together to form a ball.

2. Transfer the dough to a lightly floured surface and shape it into a flat disk. Wrap it in plastic wrap and refrigerate it for at least 1 hour or up to overnight. (The dough can be frozen for up to a month; thaw in the refrigerator before using.)

From the Kitchen of
Jessica Kartalija
Channel 13 WJZ-TV
News Anchor/Reporter

Red Pepper Pasta
With Sausage

Ingredients

- 4 Italian sausages

- 2 cloves minced garlic

- 2 onions

- 2½ red peppers, sliced

- ¼ cup Italian parsley

- ¼ cup fresh basil, chopped

- 1 tsp black pepper

- One 16 oz can of tomato sauce

- 1 cup Parmesan cheese

- ¼ cup Parmesan cheese
  (for topping cooked pasta)

- ¼ cup heavy whipping cream

Instructions

1. Crumble sausage into large skillet. Cook in olive oil with garlic.

2. Add peppers, onions and black pepper. Cook until onion is transparent.

3. Add basil, parsley, cream, tomato sauce and Parmesan cheese. Cook until thick.

4. Add mixture to pasta.

5. Top individual dishes with additional Parmesan cheese.

From the Kitchen of
Maryland Governor Martin O'Malley

Crab Cakes
From the O'Malley Family

Ingredients

- 1 lb Jumbo Lump Crab, well picked
- 1 egg, well beaten
- ½ cup mayonnaise
- 1 Tbsp lemon juice
- 1 tsp Worcestershire Sauce
- ½ tsp powdered mustard
- 7 saltine crackers, crushed
- 1/8 tsp cayenne pepper
- 1 Tbsp chopped parsley
- ½ tsp Old Bay® Seasoning

Instructions

1. Mix together all ingredients except crab.

2. Fold in crab.

3. Press into 6 cakes and place on buttered sheet pan.

4. Bake at 400° for 10-15 minutes, until golden.

From the Kitchen of
Adam May
Channel 13 WJZ-TV
News Anchor/Reporter

Tater-Tot Hot Dish

Ingredients

- 1 lb ground beef/turkey
- ¼ cup diced onion
- Small can sliced mushrooms (optional)
- 2 cans cream of mushroom soup
- 2 cups shredded cheese
- 1 package frozen tater-tots

Instructions

1. Brown and season ground beef with diced onion and mushrooms. Pour mixture into 9" x 13" glass baking dish.

2. Top with soup and cheese and arrange frozen tater-tots in single layer.

3. Cover with foil. Bake for 1 hour at 325° or until bubbling and browned.

Oriental Hot Dish

Ingredients

- 1 lb ground beef/chicken
- 1 cup raw rice
- ¼ cups diced onion
- 2 cups diced celery
- 1 can cream of mushroom soup
- 1 can cream of chicken soup
- 2 tsp butter
- 2 cups water
- ¼ cup soy sauce
- 1 can bean sprouts
- Crunchy Chinese noodles (optional)

Instructions

1. Brown and season ground beef with diced onion.

2. Mix in remaining ingredients and pour into 9" x 13" glass baking dish.

3. Bake 1.5 hours at 350°. Top with optional crunchy Chinese noodles.

"Nothing is better on a cold day than one of my Mother's casseroles, affectionately called a 'Hot Dish' in her native Minnesota. They are easy to cook, great for kids and delicious as leftovers. I'm still working on a perfect crab hot dish recipe so I can add some Maryland flavor. Enjoy!"

**-Adam May, Channel 13
WJZ-TV News Anchor/Reporter**

From the Kitchen of
Vic Carter
Channel 13 WJZ-TV
News Anchor

Vic's Limoncello Old Bay® Shrimp With Angel Hair Pasta

Ingredients

- ½ box of Angel Hair pasta
- Salt
- 40 large shrimp
- Old Bay® Seasoning to taste
- 2 Tbsp olive oil
- 1 tsp unsalted butter
- ½ medium onion, peeled and sliced
- 1 clove garlic, minced
- 3 lemons
- ¼ cup Limoncello Liqueur
- ½ cup chicken stock
- 1 Tbsp chopped parsley, fresh or dried

Instructions

1. Cook Angel Hair pasta for 4 minutes in boiling salted water. Drain pasta, reserving 1/8 cup of pasta water.

2. Peel and devein shrimp. Coat with Old Bay® Seasoning and set aside.

3. Using a Microplane®, remove the zest from two lemons and set aside.

4. Juice all of the lemons and set aside.

5. Add olive oil and onions to heated pan. Sauté until translucent.

6. Add garlic and half of the lemon zest. Sauté for a few seconds, then add half of the lemon juice.

7. Add shrimp and sauté until nearly done, turning once.

8. Add Limoncello Liqueur and light to flambé. Douse flames with remaining lemon juice and stock.

9. Add previously drained 1/8 cup of pasta water to the shrimp. Toss in the pasta.

10. Sprinkle with fresh or dried parsley to taste.

11. Serve Immediately.

Desserts

From the Kitchen of
Dolly Parton

Islands In The Stream

Ingredients

- 3 eggs, separated

- 2/3 cup sugar

- 2 heaping tsp flour

- 1 quart milk

- 1 tsp vanilla

- Nutmeg (optional)

Instructions

1. Cream egg yolks with sugar and whip until smooth, add flour and mix well. Scald the milk and when hot enough, add the cream mixture. Stir constantly 20-25 minutes until it thickens. Remove from heat and add vanilla.

2. Boil some water. Whip egg whites and add to water until hardened. Remove with spatula and put on top of the cream mixture. Sprinkle with nutmeg. Chill.

American Red Cross

Blood Type O is the most requested by hospitals.

From the Kitchen of
Arnold Schwarzenegger
Governor of California

Governor Schwarzenegger's Kaiserschmarren

Serves 2-3 as a dessert

Ingredients

- 2 whole eggs

- 1 egg white

- Pinch of salt

- 4 Tbsp flour

- 2-3 Tbsp milk or cream

- 2 Tbsp raisins, preferably soaked in light or dark rum for 15 minutes, then drained

- 2 Tbsp butter (total)

- Powdered sugar for dusting

- Cranberry sauce or berry preserves

Instructions

1. Preheat oven to 400°.

2. Break egg and egg white into a mixing bowl. Beat with a wire whisk until well-blended and foamy. Whisk in salt, flour and milk or cream. Beat well, adding additional milk by driblets until a smooth batter is achieved.

3. Add batter to a medium non-stick frying pan over medium heat. In the batter melt 1 Tbsp of butter and place in the center of the oven.

4. When bottom of pancake is golden brown, flip it over with a spatula. Immediately place frying pan in preheated oven.

5. In 4-5 minutes, remove pan from oven. Pancake will have puffed slightly.

6. Using two rubber spatulas or wooden spoons, and leaving pancake pieces against one pan, tear it into rough bite-sized pieces. Push pancake pieces against one side of the pan. Place pan back on a burner over medium heat.

7. In the "empty" half of frying pan, melt the remaining 1 Tbsp butter, and then sprinkle the 2 Tbsp sugar over the butter, and let it bubble for a minute or two.

8. Quickly toss the torn-up pancake with the cooked butter and sugar, then turn out onto serving plates. Dust with powdered sugar and serve with preserves on the side.

"This Austrian oven-baked pancake with raisins, served with powdered sugar and preserves, is truly a scrumptious treat that my family and I enjoy!"

-Governor Arnold Schwarzenegger

Thanks for all
your hard work
Love Cleaver
Barbara Billingsley

From the Kitchen of
Barbara Billingsley

June Cleaver's Brownies

Ingredients

- 1 stick butter

- 1 stick margarine

- 4 squares of baking chocolate

- 2 cups sugar

- 4 eggs

- 1 cup flour

- 2 tsp vanilla

- 1 to 1½ cups pecan pieces

- 1 generous cup chopped milk chocolate or chocolate chips

Instructions

1. Set oven to 350°. Butter 9" x 13" glass baking dish.

2. Melt butter, margarine and chocolate together in a pot over low heat.

3. Turn off heat and stir in sugar.

4. Add eggs one at a time, beating until blended.

5. Stir in flour and vanilla, then nuts.

6. Smooth in dish and sprinkle chocolate bits over top.

7. Bake 30 minutes.

8. Cool in pan, then cut into pieces as desired.

Variations: Omit nuts and use mint flavored chocolate chips on top. Or sprinkle nuts on top with chocolate bits. Or omit chocolate on top and when brownies are cool, frost with a vanilla butter cream icing and glaze with melted chocolate.

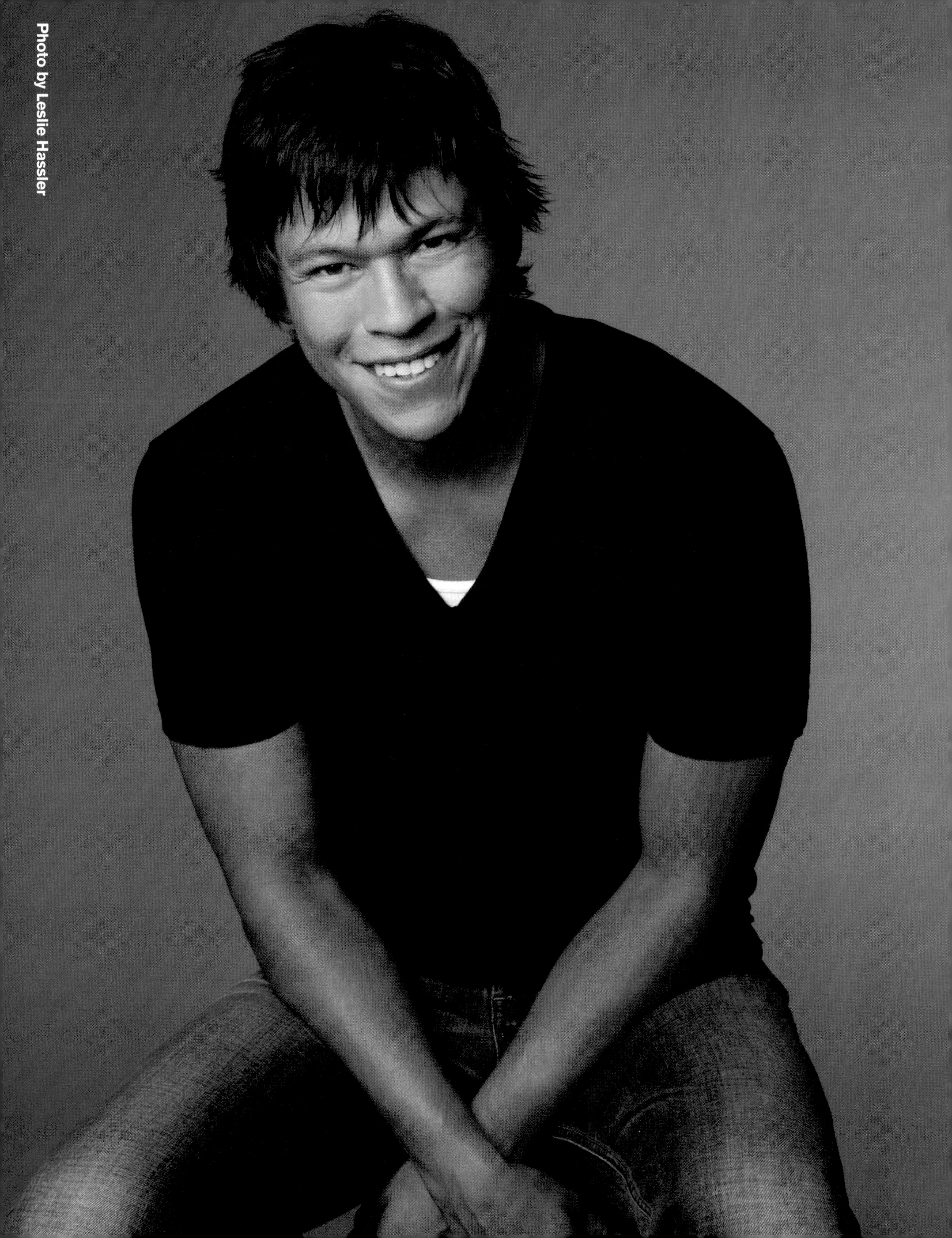

Photo by Leslie Hassler

From the Kitchen of
Chaske Spencer

Chaske Apple Pear Pie

Ingredients

- 3 peeled Granny Smith Apples
- 3 peeled pears
- Cinnamon
- Sugar
- ½ Lemon
- Pre-made pie crust

Instructions

1. Preheat oven to 375°.
2. Slice fruit and place in pie crust.
3. Squeeze ½ lemon over fruit.
4. Sprinkle cinnamon and sugar to taste.
5. Place top crust on pie.
6. Bake 45 minutes to 1 hour at 375°.

American Red Cross

97% of us will either need blood, or know someone who needs blood in our lifetimes.

From the Kitchen of
Jack & Elaine LaLanne

Apples "LaLa"

Ingredients

- Apples that have been cored

- 1 Tbsp per apple of honey

- 1/8 tsp or to taste of cinnamon

Instructions

1. Mix honey and cinnamon together and pour into the center of each apple.

2. Bake at 350°. Time varies depending on size of apple (bake large apples for 35 minutes).

3. Use the leftover honey and cinnamon and drizzle over apples.

"When Jack and I were first dating, I was a single mother raising two small children on my own. We didn't dine out very much so Jack would come over to my home and cook our meals from time to time. I was still adjusting to my new lifestyle of healthy eating and Jack, who is an amazing chef, would make us these incredibly delicious meals. One of them is 'Apples LaLa.' Enjoy!"

-The LaLannes
www.jacklalanne.com

From the Kitchen of
Natasha Barrett
Talk Show Host/Reporter
WJLA-TV, Washington, DC

Knedli (Ka-NED-lee)

Ingredients

- 6 white potatoes
- 12 prunes
- 1 egg
- Approximately 1 cup of all-purpose flour, more if needed
- Two sticks of butter
- Panko bread crumbs

Instructions

1. Boil potatoes.
2. Peel potatoes.
3. Mash potatoes.
4. Put one raw egg in the mashed potatoes.
5. Add a pinch of salt.
6. Put flour in as needed to form the dough.
7. Spread it like pizza dough.
8. Cut the dough in squares big enough for a prune.
9. Now, for the prunes: Take the pit out of each prune. Cut each prune in half. Put a spoonful of sugar in each prune half. Then, cover each prune half in dough making a ball. Boil dough balls in a pot of water until they pop up in the surface of the water.
10. The topping: In a separate smaller pot melt butter with bread crumbs. Brown the crumbs a little bit.
11. Drip the butter and bread crumbs on top of each plum.
12. Add as much sugar as you like on top and serve.

"As a little girl I would beg my Mom to make Knedli for me. This is my favorite dessert that I grew up making and eating every chance I could. The taste and smell remind me of home and it brings me back to the kitchen I was raised in.

My mother was born and raised in Zagreb, Croatia. Knedli is an authentic dish she grew up making with her mother as well. My Grandmother passed it down to us."

-Natasha Barrett, Talk Show Host and Reporter at WJLA-TV in Washington, DC

From the Kitchen of

Gary J. Ouellette

CEO, American Red Cross
Greater Chesapeake & Potomac
Blood Services Region

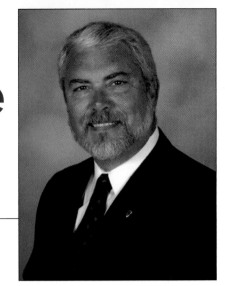

Fantastic Cheesecake

Ingredients

Crust

- 1 pack of graham crackers, finely crushed
- ½ stick of margarine, melted
- ¼ cup of sugar

Filling

- Two 8 oz packages of softened cream cheese
- 1 cup of sugar
- 3 eggs
- 1 pint sour cream
- 1 tsp vanilla

Instructions

1. Crust: Mix together crushed graham crackers, melted margarine and sugar. Press mixture into a spring bottom pan.

2. Filling: Combine cream cheese, sugar, eggs (added one at a time), sour cream and vanilla. Mix until smooth and pour into pan.

3. Bake in preheated 350° oven for 30 minutes. Turn off oven and leave cheesecake in for at least one hour.

4. Top with favorite fruit and ENJOY!

"Let my recipe be a reminder of how sweet it is to save a life. 97% of us will either need blood or know someone who needs it in our lifetimes. That's almost all of us. Please come back and donate again when you are eligible. Blood donors are heroes!"

-Gary J. Ouellette, CEO
Greater Chesapeake & Potomac Blood Services Region

From the Kitchen of
Sarah Fleischer
98 Rock, Weekday Morning DJ

Tomato Tart With Olives and Cheese
Serves 8

Ingredients

- 10" deep dish pastry shell
- 2 medium tomatoes, sliced thick
- 1 ¼ tsp salt
- ¼ cup flour
- ¼ tsp freshly ground pepper
- 2 Tbsp olive oil
- ½ cup sliced Kalamata Olives
- ¼ cup minced green onions
- 3 oz provolone cheese, thinly sliced
- 2 eggs, slightly beaten
- 1 cup grated cheddar cheese
- 1 cup heavy cream

Instructions

1. Prick pastry shell with fork. Bake at 425° for 12 minutes. Remove from oven and set aside. Reduce oven to 375°.

2. Sprinkle tomato slices with ½ tsp salt and drain on paper towels for 15 minutes, turning once.

3. Mix together the ¼ cup flour, ¾ tsp salt and ¼ tsp pepper.

4. Dip tomato slices in flour mixture and sauté briefly in olive oil, being careful not to let tomatoes fall apart.

5. Line pastry shell with olives, onions and provolone cheese. Top with tomato slices.

6. Combine eggs, cheddar cheese and heavy cream. Pour over pie.

7. Bake 45 minutes or until set. Cool 5 minutes before slicing. Serve warm or at room temperature.

For a reduced fat version: Substitute ½ cup pasteurized egg substitute plus 1 egg white for the eggs; Reduced fat cheddar cheese for the cheddar; Evaporated skim milk for the heavy cream.

Mary Yep
American Red Cross Supporter

Peanut Butter Chip Chocolate Chip Peanut Butter Cookies
Makes 40 cookies

Ingredients

- One 14 oz can sweetened condensed milk

- ¾ cup peanut butter

- 1 tsp vanilla

- 2 cups Bisquick® or baking mix

- 1 cup peanut butter chips/chocolate chips total

- ½ cup sugar

Instructions

1. Mix sweetened condensed milk, peanut butter, and vanilla together.

2. Mix in Bisquick® or baking mix.

3. Stir in peanut butter chips/chocolate chips.

4. Portion into 1 Tbsp balls. Roll in sugar. Place on cookie sheets 1" apart.

5. Bake in preheated 350° oven for 6-8 minutes. Cool on cookie sheets 1 minute. Remove from cookie sheets to cooling racks.

If you began donating blood at age 17 and donated every 56 days until you reached 76, you would have donated 48 gallons of blood, potentially helping save more than 1,000 lives!

From the Kitchen of

Stephanie Snowden
American Red Cross Staff

Mama's Banana Pound Cake

Ingredients

- 3 cups of all-pupose flour
- 3 cups of sugar
- 6 eggs
- 1 cup of evaporated milk
- 1 lb of butter (melted)
- 1 box Jell-O® Instant Banana Pudding
- 1 Tbsp of vanilla flavor
- 1 Tbsp of baking powder
- Pinch of salt

Instructions

1. Preheat oven to 350°.

2. Combine all ingredients together and pour into a bundt cake baking pan.

3. Bake for 1 hour.

From the Kitchen of

Donna Sword
American Red Cross Staff

Gramma Walker's Apple Tea Ring

Ingredients

- 3 Tbsp sugar
- ¾ tsp salt
- 3 Tbsp shortening
- ¾ cup milk (scalded)
- 1 cake yeast
- 1 egg (well beaten)
- 2½ cups sifted flour
- 1 Tbsp melted butter
- 3 Tbsp sugar
- 1 tsp cinnamon
- 3 Tbsp chopped walnuts
- 1 cup diced apples

Instructions

1. Add sugar, salt and shortening to scalded milk and cool to lukewarm.

2. Soften yeast in a little lukewarm milk and add to milk mixture. Add egg. Sift flour and add to yeast mixture in about two portions, mixing to make a soft dough. Knead for 5 minutes. Place in greased bowl. Cover and let rise in warm place (80-85 degrees) until doubles in bulk, about 1 hour and 45 minutes.

3. Roll out into a rectangle until 12" long by 10" wide. Brush with melted butter.

4. Combine last 4 ingredients (sugar, cinnamon, walnuts and apples). Spread on dough. Roll up and put ends together. Let rise until double, about 45 minutes. Cut and turn sideways.

5. Bake at 375° for 30 minutes.

Mary Ellen Oravetz
Platelet Donor

Pumpkin Roll

Ingredients

Pumpkin Roll
- 3 eggs (beat)
- ¾ cup sugar
- 2/3 cup canned pumpkin (not pumpkin pie mix)
- 1 tsp baking soda
- 1 tsp cinnamon (heaping)
- ¾ cup flour

Filling
- 8 oz cream cheese
- 1½ tsp margarine
- 1 tsp vanilla
- 1 cup powdered sugar

Instructions

1. Pumpkin Roll: Mix ingredients in order with spoon.

2. Grease 15½" x 10½" x 1" cookie sheet (or jelly roll pan) with butter/margarine.

3. Line pan with wax paper. Grease wax paper with butter/margarine. Pour batter onto wax paper. Sprinkle with nuts (optional).

4. Bake at 375° for 15 minutes or less. Turn out on damp dish towel sprinkled with powdered sugar. Roll in towel let cool.

5. Filling: Cream ingredients together. Unroll the roll and spread on filling. Roll up and refrigerate.

Matthew Weaver
Double Red Cell Donor

English Toffee

Ingredients
- 1¼ cups butter
- 1 and 2/3 cup sugar
- 1¼ cup water
- 1 tsp salt
- 4 Tbsp Karo® Lite Syrup
- 8 Hershey's® Chocolate bars
- 1 cup chopped pecans

Instructions

1. Melt butter, sugar, water and salt in a saucepan. Add in Karo® Lite Syrup and continue to stir until dissovled. Continue to stir until a temp of 300° (You can use a hard candy thermometer). It will thicken up and boil, be careful to not let it burn. It can take between 30-40 minutes, watch carefully and stir frequently. While waiting, cut pecans and break up candy bars. Butter a cookie sheet to spread the toffee on.

2. Once at desired temperature, turn heat off and add half the pecans. Pour toffee on the cookie sheet, it will spread out naturally. Let sit for a couple of minutes then add chocolate on top. It will soften, then spread across toffee with end of a spoon. Sprinkle the rest of chopped pecans on top of the chocolate.

3. Place toffee in freezer for about 30 minutes, then break into pieces. Too long in the freezer and the chocolate will pop off the toffee, so be sure to monitor, as all freezer temps are different. Store in the freezer until ready to serve. Enjoy!

From the Kitchen of
Cheryl Flanagan
American Red Cross Staff

The American Red Cross blood program started in 1940, under the leadership of Dr. Charles Drew.

Tom's Apple Pie
For Pat Preston

Ingredients

- 2 Pillsbury® rolled pie crusts
- 6 very large Granny Smith apples
- ¾ cup sugar
- ¾ tsp cinnamon
- ¼ tsp nutmeg
- 2 Tbsp flour
- 1/8 tsp salt
- 1 Tbsp lemon juice, and the zest of the lemon
- ½ stick butter
- ¼ cup honey

Instructions

1. Preheat oven to 425°. Place one of the crusts in a 10" glass pie plate and reserve second crust for top.

2. In a large bowl, peel and roughly chop the apples and add the lemon juice and zest.

3. In smaller bowl mix the next 5 ingredients and add to the apple lemon mixture. Place the apple mixture in the pie crust.

4. Dot apples with ½ stick of butter and cover with remaining crust. Flute edges and with a sharp knife and make 5 slits in the top.

5. Warm ¼ cup honey in a measuring cup and with a pastry brush lightly brush the top.

6. Bake for 30 minutes. Reduce heat to 350° and cook an additional 30 to 40 minutes.

7. You will probably want to tent the pie the last 20 minutes or so.

Only 7 percent of people in the U.S. have O- negative blood type. O- negative is the universal donor and can be given to people of all blood types.

From the Kitchen of
Eleanor Serich, Jonathan Papelbon's Grandmother

Dump Cake

Ingredients

- 1 can pie filling (cherry, blueberry, strawberry)
- 1 can crushed pineapple, drained
- 1 box cake mix (any flavor)
- 1¼ stick of Oleo (sliced)
- 1½ cup walnuts, chopped
- ½ cup coconut

Instructions

1. Spread pie filling in a 9" x 13" glass pan.

2. Scatter pineapple over the fruit mixture.

3. Sprinkle dry cake mix in layers over filling.

4. Drop slices of Oleo over cake mix.

5. Scatter nuts and coconut on top.

6. DO NOT STIR.

7. Bake at 350° for 40 minutes.

"Growing up, we had this cake at least once a month."

-Eleanor Serich

From the Kitchen of
Laura Fries
Blood Donor & Mother of Blood Recipient

First Snow Streusel Coffee Cake

Ingredients

Coffee Cake
- 2 cups all purpose flour
- 1 cup sugar
- 3 tsp baking powder
- 1 tsp salt
- 1/3 cup butter or margarine, softened
- 1 egg
- 1 cup of milk

Cinnamon Streusel
- 2/3 cup packed brown sugar
- 2/3 cup all purpose flour
- 1 tsp cinnamon
- 6 Tbsp firm, cold butter or margarine

Instructions

1. Heat oven to 350°. Grease 9-inch round pan.

2. In small bowl, stir streusel ingredients until crumbly; set aside. Make sure butter is very cold, or else it won't crumble properly.

3. In medium bowl, mix coffee cake ingredients until blended.

4. Spread in pan. Use half of streusel for the middle and sprinkle the other half on top.

5. Bake 35-40 minutes or until golden brown.